THE
BATTLE OF
GALVESTON

EAKIN PRESS Fort Worth, Texas
www.EakinPress.com

THE
BATTLE OF
GALVESTON

by

Tom Townsend

EAKIN PRESS ✪ Fort Worth, Texas
www.EakinPress.com

Copyright © 1989
By Tom Townsend
Published By Eakin Press
An Imprint of Wild Horse Media Group
P.O. Box 331779
Fort Worth, Texas 76163
1-817-344-7036
www.EakinPress.com

1 2 3 4 5 6 7 8 9
ISBN-10: 1-68179-029-7
ISBN-13: 978-1-68179-029-9

For Pat and Joyce

Contents

1

Cotton Bales and Cannons

December 24, 1862

A cold rain swept across Main Street in Houston. North winds lashed at the covered top of a big freight wagon, making the canvas pop and crack as it lumbered along the water-filled carriage way. Four skinny horses, knee-deep in the mud, strained in their harness to keep the wagon moving.

Along both sides of the street, soldiers marched with their rifles slung muzzle down and their faces lowered against the weather. Their coats of faded gray and chestnut brown were as soaked as the ground they trod. Many walked with blankets covering their heads and shoulders.

Luke Cochrane sat beside his father on the wagon seat. His old hat was pulled down low and the turned-up collar of his patched, wool coat completely hid his dark, curly hair. Candles on a Christmas tree in a store win-

1

dow caught his eye as the wagon passed. He shivered against the cold. Somehow, this did not seem much like Christmas Eve.

For Luke, the Civil War had come suddenly to the Texas coast three months ago when the Yankee navy had blockaded Galveston. Since then, even the most common things, like clothes and medicine, had become expensive and hard to find. Several regiments of the Confederate army were now camped here, in Houston, some sixty miles north of Galveston. Everyone believed that it was only a matter of time before the Yankees would land troops and move north.

Luke's father watched as the soldiers passed. It was odd, he thought, that so many of them would be moving on Christmas Eve. "Yep," he commented idly, "sure does look like that new General Magruder is up ta somethin'."

"You reckon he can run them Yankees outa Galveston, Pa?" Luke asked, looking up into the weathered face of his father. Jake Cochrane's hair was gray now, but along his bushy sideburns and mustache were still a few streaks of sandy brown. Fifty years of life on the rugged Texas coast had dimmed, but not extinguished, the twinkle in his brown eyes.

"Don't rightly know, son," he answered as the wagon jolted through a deep rut and Luke held on tighter. "It'd be tough with no navy. And there sure ain't no warships up here in Houston."

"I don't see why the army wants this old cotton, anyway," Luke commented. He looked over his shoulder at the damp bales of raw, smelly cotton that filled their wagon. "It's all rotted and ain't no good."

"I don't know either, but they're payin' us good money to deliver it down to Allen's Landing, so I reckon they got something in mind for it."

Most all of the cotton left in Texas was just as rotten as the bales in the Cochranes' wagon. It had been picked in the fall, and then, when the Yankees blockaded Galveston, there had been no way for it to be shipped. Thou-

2

sands of ruined bales were now piled on the docks at Houston. Luke could not understand. Why did the army want more?

Main Street ended at Buffalo Bayou. Ahead, Luke could see the docks at Allen's Landing. Steamboats were moored along the tree-lined banks. Beneath the gray afternoon sky, most of them looked old and abandoned. With the Yankee navy blockading the only deep-water entrance to Galveston Bay, all shipping had been shut down to and from Houston. In fact, almost all traffic, anywhere along the coast, was shut down. A few steamboats had retreated here, into these protected reaches of Buffalo Bayou, to avoid the guns of the blockading fleet.

A soldier stepped out and blocked their path. Two stars on the collar of his gray coat indicated that he was a lieutenant in the Confederate army. "These here bales go down to the *Neptune*," he ordered and waved them past.

Luke's father urged the team on through the mud. "The old *Neptune*," he laughed grimly. "I remember back in '53 when she raced the *Farmer* down from Harrisburg. *Farmer* blew a boiler up near Halfmoon Shoal . . . killed thirty people. We could see the fire clear back to Morgan's Point."

The wagon came to a halt beside one of the aging steamboats. Her once-white paint had faded to a dirty shade of gray. Rust had eaten holes in both her smokestacks, and her lower deck seemed to be only inches above the bayou's dirty surface. Green slime and barnacles dotted the wooden blades of the monstrous paddlewheel at her stern. The two steady streams of water being pumped over her side hinted that she was leaking badly. But wisps of smoke curled in the wind above her stacks, and the red glow from her firebox was visible through the open engine room doors. The *Neptune* was preparing to go somewhere.

The decks were a beehive of activity. Soldiers and workmen swarmed about, piling cotton bales along the decks and lashing them in place. Firewood to fuel the engine was being carried aboard, along with barrels marked "GUNPOWDER." On the dock, two cannons rested on large wheeled carriages. Their long barrels were protected from the weather beneath oilcloth tarpaulins.

"Ahoy there, Jake Cochrane!" a deep voice boomed at them. Both Luke and his father looked up toward the pilothouse, where a heavy man in a dark frock coat and a high-peaked captain's hat was hailing them through a speaking trumpet. Even from this distance, his bushy, red beard was bright in the gloom.

Jake squinted his eyes through the rain. "Well, be danged if it ain't Bill Sangster," he said to Luke and then yelled up to the pilothouse. "Ahoy yourself, ya old river rat. What in the name of tarnation brings your crusty hide up the bayou here?"

"Them Yankees chased me up here!" the big voice returned. "Gunboat like ta blowed me outa the water down by Pelican Spit two weeks back. But we're fixin' ta give 'em a lickin' they'll remember fer a spell."

Jake ran his eyes over the worn-out steamboat and could not keep from laughing. "What ya gonna do — steam down ta Galveston and sink on top of 'em?"

Sangster's hearty laugh rolled across the bayou like pleasant thunder.

"You know him, Pa?" Luke asked.

There was a hint of sadness in his father's eyes when he said, "Shipped with him once or twice. Back when Texas was a republic, before we went and joined that dang-fool Union we're fightin' just ta get out of now."

Luke's eyes had gotten larger as his father spoke. "Ya never said nothin' about that before."

Jake Cochrane paused and nodded his head slowly. "Yer ma didn't much like ta hear about it, so I kept it to myself."

Luke dropped his eyes. It had been two winters since the fevers had taken his mother. He had accepted it now, but the mention of her still brought back sad memories.

5

"We was fightin' the Mexicans," Jake continued. "Texas had her own navy back then. Me and old Sangster there served on a sloop-of-war called the *Austin*."

Again the big voice called down from the *Neptune*'s hurricane deck. "Come aboard and warm your bones, Cochrane. I've a jimmyjohn of sour mash somewheres about and a spot of tea for the youngun there."

Jake waved his hand and stepped down off the wagon, followed closely by Luke. They walked up the gangplank onto the old steamer's deck and then made their way among the busy soldiers to a set of rusty iron stairs which led up to the hurricane deck.

Captain Sangster met them at the pilothouse door. He shook hands with Jake, and they stepped inside.

"I heard ya had a boy," Sangster said, slapping Jake on the back and winking a bloodshot eye at Luke.

A wooden wheel, twice as tall as Luke and banded with polished brass, stood in the center of the pilothouse. Beside it were levers and gauges. A chain with a large, shiny handle hung from the ceiling, and Luke realized that it was used to blow the whistle.

"Where you headed with all this no-good cotton and them two cannon?" Jake asked as Sangster passed him a jug of whiskey.

Sangster grinned. There was a note of excitement in his voice when he said, "Magruder is gonna attack the Yankee fleet at Galveston. As for them twenty-four-pounders, we borrowed 'em from Mosely's battery of the 13th Texas."

Luke watched his father's eyes narrow suspiciously as he passed back the jug. "All right, but what are you gonna do with this wore-out steamboat?"

Sangster's grin widened. "This here wore-out steamboat just happens to be the Confederate frigate *Neptune*. Up the dock there is another frigate, the *Bayou City*." He pointed out the starboard windows. " 'Cotton-clads' we call 'em."

"You been sippin' too much of this here sour mash," Jake said, leaning toward the window. "*Bayou City* ain't

6

nothin' but another ol' wore-out bay steamer, just a bit bigger'n this one here that's tryin' ta sink under you."

"We figure them cotton bales ought to work like armor plate. Leastways they'll get us in close enough to board."

Jake shook his head. "Jes' who is this 'we' you keep on talkin' about?"

"Me and Henry Lubbuck and Leon Smith. You remember Leon?" Sangster asked as he reached into his vest pocket and took out a crooked pipe.

Jake nodded. "Leon the Lion. It figures. He always was even crazier than you. Wasn't he the skipper when *Bayou City* blew her boiler up at Lynchburg in '59?"

"The same," Sangster said as he lit his pipe. " 'Cept now, General Magruder's made him sort of an admiral. Admiral of the Confederate Fleet of Galveston Bay, I reckon you'd call it."

Jake laughed again. "Admiral of a bunch of crazy men, all fixin' ta maybe get theirselves killed."

Luke moved close to his father and sat down on a narrow padded bench against the pilothouse wall. "Well," Jake was saying, "I'm just proud I ain't no part of this here navy, as you call it." He turned to Luke. "Come on, son. We got a wagon to unload, and a far piece to travel before dark."

They rose to leave and were nearly at the door when Sangster spoke again. "Thought you might like to come along, Jake. I sure could use me a master gunner like you for them twenty-four-pounders."

Luke felt his father's hand tighten on his shoulder. Together they turned back to face Sangster. Jake's eyes were different, Luke realized suddenly. The sparkle had become a flame he had never seen before. A long moment passed as the two men faced each other. Luke looked back and forth between his father and Captain Sangster. Each seemed to be testing the other.

It was Sangster who spoke next. His smile was gone and his voice was dead serious. "I need ya, Jake. It wasn't no accident the army hired you to haul cotton up here. I set it up."

"Not on your life," Jake answered flatly and turned to leave.

"Jake, wait," Sangster added quickly. "Look, I got three hundred men, all that's left of Sibley's Brigade back from New Mexico. They's good men, all veterans, but not one of 'em can hit the broad side of a red barn at noon with one of them twenty-fours from the deck of a rolling ship. I need me a navy gunner. Like the man who shot the flagstaff off the *Guadalupe* at the Battle of Campeche — like you, Jake."

"Sorry, Bill, that was twenty years ago," Jake answered firmly, but Luke could feel the sadness in his voice.

"I could have ya conscripted," Sangster threatened.

Jake shook his head. "I tried ta join up when my Margaret died two years back. They said I was too old."

"Law's changed. We're losin' this here war, case you ain't noticed. Federals got New Orleans, 'bout to take Vicksburg and split us right in half. Come spring, they'll be ready to enlist my old granny."

"Maybe your granny, but not me." Jake looked away.

Sangster nodded his head sadly. "It's okay Jake, I understand. But look, it's Christmas Eve. Stay aboard tonight. There's a Christmas tree down in the saloon. We're not sailin' for another day or two. Maybe I could hire ya long enough to teach a few of them young whippersnappers out there some of the finer points of naval gunnery."

Jake avoided Sangster's eyes. "I could do that. There won't be no charge," he said quietly.

Sangster's wide grin returned with disturbing speed. "I knew ya would, Jake! Heck, it'll be just like old times again."

Luke saw his father smiling and was surprised. He had never thought of him as a soldier, but now he was going to teach men how to shoot cannons. That much was easy to be proud of. But inside, Luke had the sick feeling that before it was all over, the war was going to get much too close.

2

Christmas Presents

Fog settled on Buffalo Bayou as evening came. The steamers were ghostly outlines in the gray mist — vague and out of focus. Aboard the *Neptune,* oil lamps hung from the ceiling of the saloon and filled the old ship with a warm glow. Candles burned on a little Christmas tree set up on one of the tables. A banjo plunked out the tinny strains of an old Christmas carol, and most of the soldiers were singing.

Luke remembered happier times: Christmas Eves when his mother was alive and they went to mass in the little log church near their farm at Morgan's Point. There were presents then: hard candy, fruit, and new shoes if the crops had been good. The war had changed all that. Jake had not been very interested in farming since Luke's mother died. Now he made a little money hauling freight with their wagon, and he preferred to be moving.

"Merry Christmas, son," Jake said suddenly. He

9

handed Luke a hunting knife. "Been meaning to give you this for a long time; just never got around to it."

Luke had not expected a present this year. A look of surprise was on his face as he said, "Thanks, Pa," and slipped the blade from its leather sheath.

"I carried it years ago aboard the *Austin*. It always served me well. Hope it'll do the same for you."

A single, five-pointed star was etched on the thick blade, and below it was the word "TEXAS." The hilt was heavy brass, and there was also a strip of brass along the blade's top. The handle was smooth whalebone, with a brass top.

"Just remember that it ain't no toy."

"I will, Pa," Luke promised, "and Merry Christmas." He returned the knife to its sheath and asked, "How long we gonna stay here?"

His father looked away. "Couple of days," he said. "I'll show these boys how to fire them cannon, and then we'll be headin' back to the farm. Unless we find somethin' else to haul."

Luke fondled his knife. "Pa, do you wish you was goin' with 'em?"

"Heck, boy," Jake snapped, "you teched in the head? Sangster is crazy, Leon Smith is crazier, and from everything I hear tell, this new General Magruder is crazier than both of them put together. Why they — " Luke met his father's eyes and he hesitated. "Well, maybe if I was a little younger, I might give it some thought," he admitted grudgingly and turned away.

*   *   *   *

On Christmas morning, the sun was shining. The two cannons were hoisted onto the *Neptune*'s forward deck and lashed in place with heavy ropes and chains. For the rest of the day, Jake worked with the men who had volunteered to man the cannons.

Luke sat on a cotton bale and watched as they trained. Over and over they repeated the same routine.

On the command of "Load!" one man drove a sponge, attached to a long pole, down the barrel while another brought up a powder charge, wrapped in paper. Then, using the other end of the pole, the charge was "rammed home" down the barrel. The cannonball, or round shot as they called it, followed the powder charge down the barrel. Next, a long thin spike, called a priming wire, was stuck into the small hole at the rear of the cannon, which was called the vent. This wire, Luke learned, punched a hole in the paper around the powder charge and was then removed.

Next, a device called a friction tube was attached to a length of rope called a lanyard and was inserted into the vent. When the lanyard was pulled, the friction tube made sparks which would set off the gunpowder and fire the cannon.

"Now remember to fire as the bow rises," Jake told them. "An' don't get in no rush, 'cause ya can't afford to miss. Them Yankee gunners been practicin' for years, and they ain't apt to miss more than once or twice."

"What kind of guns the *Harriet Lane* got?" one of the men asked. Everyone had heard about the fast sidewheel steamer, *Harriet Lane*. She was the pride of the Yankee fleet blockading Galveston.

"I ain't never seen her, but I hear tell she's got a thirty-two-pounder for a swivel gun forward. And it won't be no smooth-bore like these Napoleons we got. It'll be a parrot rifle; got grooves inside the barrel to make the shot spin, just like a rifle." He pointed at an army rifle standing nearby. "It'll shoot a whole lot farther and straighter than anything we got.

"And as for her main battery," Jake continued, "most likely, they're nine-inch cannons. If she hits us just once with one of them, well now, it's all over but the prayin'."

One of the men asked, "You reckon these here cotton bales gonna stop a parrot rifle?"

Jake sniffed. "These here cotton bales ain't gonna

11

stop nothing. So you boys better shoot fast and you better shoot good."

Sometime during the afternoon, a half-dozen smartly uniformed officers rode up to the *Neptune*. At their front was a tall man with dark hair, long sideburns, and a mustache. In his hat was a red plume. His spotless uniform bore the insignia of a general in the Confederate army.

"Well, looky here," said an old soldier, who was standing beside Luke as the officers dismounted. "Ol' Prince John hisself is come to pay us a call."

"Prince John?" Luke asked, screwing his face into a crooked frown.

"Yep," the soldier chuckled. "We call him that when he ain't lookin'. That there is General John Bankheart Magruder, fresh in from Virginia and chompin' at the bit ta run Yankees outa Texas."

As Luke watched, the officers disappeared into the *Neptune*'s saloon and guards were posted at the doors. The men returned to work and Luke wandered back to sit on a cotton bale. After a while, the saloon door opened and someone called out loudly; "Cochrane, Jake Cochrane!" Luke looked around and saw his father go into the saloon.

Time passed slower now. The meeting seemed to drag on for hours as Luke waited, and fidgeted, as he paced the deck.

The sun was low in the west when General Magruder again appeared on deck. To Luke's surprise, he was talking to Jake as they approached.

"This must be your son, Mr. Cochrane," the general said as he stared down at Luke.

"Yes, sir. This is Luke," Jake answered.

The general extended his hand and Luke shook it with a smile. "He looks like he'll do just fine." Magruder paused and looked at his gold pocketwatch. "I'm late for a staff meeting, so I'll leave you to work out the details. You know the time schedule," he said and turned away.

Luke suddenly felt very nervous. "What's he talkin' about?" he asked, even before the officers were off the gangplank.

Jake took his arm and guided him away from the others. "Come on, son, what I've got to say ain't for other ears." They found a quiet place on the old steamer's bow. "Yankees landed troops at Galveston last night. Near as we know, they took the city. I'm stayin' on the *Neptune* for a while longer. They need a gunner real bad and I'm the only one around."

"Then I'm stayin' too," Luke announced, sticking out his chin.

His heart sank when his father shook his head. "No, son. General's got another job for you. A very important one, and you're the only one who can do it."

"Me? What can I do?"

"It's two things really." Jake lowered his voice. "First off, the army needs our wagon to haul supplies to the railroad at Harrisburg. Then you'll ride the train south with the army."

"Then what?" Luke asked.

"The general wants you to guide one man back up to our farm and show him where our boat is. He's gonna row out from Morgan's Point and tell the ships just what time Magruder wants us to attack."

"Aw heck, Pa. Then I'm gonna be stuck back there at the farm and miss seeing them Yankees get run off." Luke pouted.

Jake's voice was stern. "You doggone right about that, boy. I want you to stay at the farm till this mess is all over with. I'll get the wagon and come home soon as I can."

Luke stared at the deck. "Look here, son," Jake went on, "General gave you an important job to do and you got to do it. These here ships have got to know just when the fight is gonna start. General Magruder don't know just yet what time he can get his men into position for an attack. But the only way he's got a chance of winning is if

13

these ships attack at just the same time and keep those Yankee gunboats busy. You understand that?"

Luke nodded his head. "Yes, sir, I reckon I do. But I sure wish I was going with you."

"Son, if it weren't for General Magruder needin' a guide, you'd be hightailin' it back home right now," Jake told him sternly. "I want you just as far away from this fight as can be."

"Shoot, Pa, this here war is gonna be over before I get old enough ta fight Yankees."

Jake grunted. "I sure hope that's the way it's gonna be."

"How come you're going with them?" Luke asked after a pause.

"Reckon it's my duty," Jake said thoughtfully. "I could probably get out of it, 'cause of my age and all, but heck, we gonna all go broke and starve to death if we can't get the Yankees out of Galveston. With that port closed up, nothing goes in or out of this whole part of Texas. That means there ain't gonna be nothing for us to haul with our wagon and nobody to buy the crops we grow. Likewise, we ain't going to be able to get nothing at the stores unless it's made right here." He shook his head in disgust. "There just don't seem to be any other way."

Luke nodded and understood. "You keep yer head down, Pa, and be real careful. Ya hear?"

3

March Order

General Magruder's army marched east toward Harrisburg three days later. The first hint of dawn was only a pink streak in the eastern sky, and a north wind whipped across Buffalo Bayou as Luke and Jake hitched up their team and wagon. Luke climbed up onto the high seat, took the reins, and separated them carefully between his fingers. Suddenly, the wagon and the team looked very big, even though he had driven them many times before.

Jake stepped up onto the wheel beside him and reached under the seat. He took out a bundle and began to unwrap it. "Reckon I better take this along," he said casually as he uncovered a heavy Colt navy revolver and slipped it into his belt. "General says for you to report to a mess sergeant named Boudreaux." Luke wrinkled his nose to show that he did not understand. "That means he's the man in charge of the cooks. I reckon you gonna be haulin' vittles."

"I got it." Luke nodded.

"You take care now, boy."

"You too, Pa," Luke answered nervously and tried to smile.

"I will. And I'll see ya at home in a week or so."

As the wagon pulled up the hill from the wharves at Allen's Landing, Luke took one last look over his shoulder at the two old river steamers, *Neptune* and *Bayou City*, as they lay moored along the bank.

The *Bayou City* was the larger of the two and looked a little bit like a real warship. She was a sidewheeler. Her high pilothouse had been removed and her wheel was relocated inside a little pen of cotton bales, just forward of the cabins. More cotton bales, piled two high, protected both her main and upper decks. On her bow was a single, thirty-two-pounder field gun.

The *Neptune* was smaller and still looked like nothing more than an old bay steamer which was overloaded with a deck cargo of cotton. Only the two cannon on her bow gave her any resemblance to a ship of war.

Luke wondered if he would ever see his father again. He brushed away a single tear, set his jaw grimly, and stared ahead as he drove the wagon off down the street.

* * * *

Soldiers were everywhere as Luke approached the big, two-story house owned by W. R. Baker, which General Magruder was using as his headquarters in Houston. He brought the team to a careful halt beside some other wagons near a cooking fire. The smells of wood smoke and bacon drifted on the morning wind. He set the brake and started to climb down off the seat when a tall man with black hair stopped him.

"What you think you're doing with that wagon, boy?" the man asked.

"Lookin' for Sergeant Boudreaux," Luke answered and frowned at the man.

"So what you want him for? He is a very busy man, trying to feed all these men three times a day." The

16

man's eyes were dark and small, his black hair was slicked neatly back, and his uniform was hidden beneath a white apron.

"I got a wagon for him to use," Luke explained.

At that statement, the man seemed astonished. "You that, what's his name . . . Cochrane? Now I know why we are losing this war. They send them to me younger every day. How old are you, boy?"

Luke stuck out his chin. "Thirteen — well, nearly."

The man grunted and said, "Well, I am Sergeant Boudreaux."

"And I'm Luke Cochrane. This here's Pa's wagon. He's stayin' on the *Neptune*."

Sergeant Boudreaux nodded thoughtfully at that remark and then said, "Pull the wagon up a little. We are going to load those barrels there." He pointed to some large wooden containers sitting nearby. "They are full of salt pork."

At Sergeant Boudreaux's command, several men began rolling the barrels to Luke's wagon. A ramp was made from a couple of boards and, one by one, the barrels were rolled up onto the wagon. When they had finished, the sergeant told Luke to follow his cook wagon, and the procession started out.

The road wound its way east, along Buffalo Bayou. Soldiers marched beside them as the wagons bumped and jolted their way through deep ruts full of rainwater and mud. Time and again the soldiers had to push the wagons on their way.

A distant steam whistle echoed along the road as they neared Harrisburg. Luke smelled smoke and cinders as he saw the railroad depot at Harrisburg just ahead. Beside it sat a steam locomotive with a long train of flatcars and boxcars. Ahead of the locomotive was a single flatcar with a cannon on it. Everywhere was excitement as soldiers hurried to climb aboard.

The wagons were quickly unloaded and Sergeant Boudreaux assured Luke that he would take good care of his horses. Luke found himself a place to sit among the soldiers crowded on one of the flatcars. By mid-morning, the train was moving slowly south.

"You comin' along ta whup up on them Yankees with us?" a tall corporal with blond hair asked Luke. Several men laughed.

"I reckon the general had to send him along just to protect you," another man chimed in.

Luke laughed too. They shared beef jerky and dried peas that the soldiers called "goobers" as the train chugged and clanked its way steadily southward. Sometime in the afternoon, they stopped near a brickyard where a few scattered houses were strung out along the tracks.

A salt-scented breeze drifted across the marsh land as the train clattered to a stop. In the distance, sea gulls circled lazily against the blue sky. Luke knew that the ocean could not be far away. Groves of salt cedars dotted the higher places, but elsewhere the ground was soft and swampy.

"Cochrane, Luke Cochrane!" He heard his own name called as a soldier came hurrying down along the train.

"I'm Luke," he said, surprised.

"Come with me, boy," the soldier ordered. "The general hisself wants to talk to you." As the astonished soldiers watched, Luke hurried off behind the man. They halted near the engine where a small group of officers in gray uniforms were gathered. Immediately, Luke recognized General Magruder. Luke waited quietly and, in a minute, the other officers saluted and left hurriedly.

"Partridge!" the general bellowed, looking around. "Where in blue blazes is that Lieutenant Partridge?"

A young man with glasses and red hair came running up, dressed in a poor-fitting uniform with a single gold star on each collar. It occurred to Luke that the lieutenant could not be more than a couple of years older than himself.

Ten yards from the general, the young lieutenant

18

tripped over a clump of salt grass and fell flat on his face. Luke had to force himself not to laugh as the lieutenant picked himself up, replaced his glasses, and finally untangled his sword belt.

"S-s-sir! L-l-lieutenant Partridge, reporting as ordered, sir!" he stammered.

The general shook his head and ignored Partridge as he turned to Luke. "Your father tells me you have a small boat at your farm on Morgan's Point. I want you to take Lieutenant Partridge to it. I've given him the exact time of our attack, and he must deliver the information to Captain Smith on the *Bayou City*. The fleet should pass Morgan's Point day after tomorrow. Can you do that?"

"I reckon so, General," Luke gulped. "Steamboats always pass close to shore at Morgan's Point 'cause the water is deepest there. Pa and me used to fish out there all the time before the war."

"Good," Magruder said and then turned to Partridge. "Get him a good horse."

"Yes, sir, right away, sir," Partridge snapped. He made an awkward salute and managed to hurry away without falling over anything else.

General Magruder turned back to Luke and knelt down on one knee to meet his eyes. "This is an important mission you and the lieutenant have. If Captain Smith doesn't get his ships into position and attack at just the same time as my army does, we don't have much chance of beating those Yankees.

"Now, Partridge there can't find the outhouse in full moonlight, but he's all I can spare. So it's mostly up to you. Do you understand, Luke?"

Luke's eyes widened and he gulped again. "Yes, sir, I reckon I'll do my best."

The general rose to his feet. "Good boy," he said, just as Partridge returned, leading another horse.

General Magruder mounted his own chestnut stallion and rode off. Partridge waited impatiently as Luke shortened the stirrups on the McClellen saddle. "Got to get my gear off the train," Luke said as he mounted and started riding back down beside the train.

Reining his horse beside the flatcar, Luke picked up his small knapsack and was reaching for his bedroll when the corporal said, "Be careful now, Luke, and keep that chicken lieutenant from messin' everything up."

Partridge puffed up and turned red. He opened his mouth to speak, but nothing came out. Finally, he just seemed to wilt.

Luke waved at the corporal and rode off. Again, he felt very lonely. He hated this war. It was separating him from everything that was his: his father and now their wagon and team. He wondered if he would ever see them again. He dug his heels into the horse's flanks, spurred him into a full gallop, and left Lieutenant Partridge to follow in his tracks.

4

Old Ben

A half-mile down the tracks, Luke brought his horse to a walk and Partridge immediately caught up with him. "You shouldn't go running off like that. We have to stay together," Partridge said.

Luke ignored him.

"You look awful young to be in this war," Partridge noted, with his nose in the air.

Luke shot him an unpleasant look. "I reckon you do too."

Partridge huffed. "I was an upperclassman at Virginia Military Academy, I'll have you know. The Southern army needed good officers in a hurry when the hostilities broke out. So, of course, I was promoted immediately. Just as soon as my father, Col. Beauregard Partridge, spoke to the governor." He looked at Luke as if the mention of his father's name should mean something. Luke just stared blankly at him and so he continued.

"Well, it doesn't matter. You just stay out of the way and I'll take care of everything."

Luke shook his head and said nothing. He wondered how many officers like Partridge the Confederate army had, and if it had anything to do with why they were losing the war.

They followed the railroad tracks as far north as Clear Creek. Luke had urged his horse into the shallow water when Partridge called out to him. "Hold up there. It's shorter if we follow this creek to the bay and then cross."

"Might be shorter," Luke sighed, "but ya can't cross there. The water's deep and the tide runs too fast."

Partridge shook his head and waved a piece of paper. "I have a map here. It plainly shows a ferry crossing there."

"There ain't no ferry crossing Clear Creek," Luke told him.

"But this is the latest army map. It has to be correct."

Luke turned his horse in midstream and slowly walked it back to the bank. "There ain't no ferry," he said in Partridge's face. "What there might be is one ol' man with a boat, but he don't like nobody. Now, if the fishin' ain't no good, and he just happens to be around, he might take me across 'cause Pa and me talk to him sometimes. But he ain't never seen you before, and when he does, he ain't gonna like what he sees."

Partridge sniffed. "This whole country is under martial law. The army is in control here, so I shall simply order him to transport us across."

"Most likely, he'll just shoot you as soon as he sees that uniform."

"You mean he's a Yankee?" Partridge gasped, looking a little pale.

"Nope," Luke answered honestly. "Ol' Ben just don't know one uniform from another and don't much care.

Some folks say he used to be a pirate. He still thinks all uniforms are Spanish."

Partridge swallowed hard and turned his horse toward the mouth of Clear Creek. "I'll deal with that riff-raff if he shows himself," he said with one hand patting his revolver.

They followed the trail east along the south bank of Clear Creek during the afternoon. Large groves of trees shaded the water's edge, and the trail was cut by several small streams. The sun was low in the west when the trail at last turned down onto a sand bar near the creek's mouth. Sea gulls circled them, squawking noisily, and the waters of Galveston Bay stretched out to the east as far as the eye could see.

Partridge guided his horse out into the water and the swift current swirled around its legs. The horse almost stumbled before the young officer turned him back to the bank. "It's too deep. We shall have to find the ferry."

Luke pointed out onto the bay. "There's a sail to the northeast. Most likely that's him out fishing. Probably won't be back until morning." He dismounted and began unsaddling his horse. "I reckon we'll camp here tonight."

"We don't have time," Partridge snapped. "We have to press on."

"I don't see how we can, unless you want to ride all the way back to the railroad bridge. Most likely, we'd get lost in the dark if we did."

Partridge continued to study his map while Luke started a fire with flint and steel from his knapsack. When it was burning well, he took out a small coil of fishing line and used his new knife to cut a pole from a nearby tree. By the time the sun had set, he had caught two fat, speckled trout and had them cooking Indian-style on stakes over the fire. When they were done, he offered one to Partridge.

The young officer sniffed at the fish and stared into its sightless eyes. "I have my army rations," he said and started to hand back the fish.

23

"So do I, but fresh-caught trout cooked over an open fire is a heck of a lot better'n hardtack and jerky."

Reluctantly, Partridge took one of the fish and picked at it cautiously until at least part of it was eaten. They laid out their bedrolls near the fire as the moon rose. The bay sparkled in its pale yellow light and the fire cast ghostly shadows on the beach. The horses whinnied nervously in the trees behind them. Luke snuggled deeper into his blankets as a cold breeze blew in from the water. Somewhere to the south, a coyote was howling.

"You say this Ben used to be a pirate?" Partridge asked suddenly. "I never heard of pirates up here."

"Yep," Luke answered sleepily and yawned. "My pa says there used to be a bunch of them. Down at Galveston, you can still see the old fort they built. Folks say Ben buried treasure somewhere up around here and stayed around to be sure no one digs it up."

"Humph," Partridge scoffed. "I doubt if there's been a pirate in these parts for forty years."

Luke saw no reason to argue the point and turned his back to the fire.

He was half-asleep when the sound of hoarse breathing awakened him, and he looked quickly in Partridge's direction. Luke blinked his eyes in disbelief. He could not see the moon. Instead he saw the huge, black silhouette of a man standing over the lieutenant's bedroll. Luke reached for his knife, just as Partridge began to scream.

5

Gators

Cold moonlight reflected off the curved blade of a cutlass as the big shadow suddenly jerked Partridge from his bedroll.

"Spanish dog! Ye come snoopin' for me treasure, have ye now?" The voice was rough and gravelly. "Maybe I'll just be cuttin' off one of your ears so as to make ye remember not to do it again."

Partridge was making loud blubbering noises as the figure dropped him back onto the sand and raised his blade.

"That ain't no Spaniard, Ben," Luke interrupted quickly. The man stopped in midair. "An' he ain't here to steal no treasure. We just need to get across the creek."

"Luke? Luke Cochrane?" the voice coughed. "What brings ye out here and where be your father?"

"He sort of joined the navy, I reckon. There's gonna be a big battle at Galveston ta run the Yankees out. We got ta get up to Morgan's Point real fast."

The dark figure hesitated and then said, "Aye, Luke, I'll take ye across soon as I cut off the ears of this Spanish dog here."

Partridge began scrambling away on his hands and knees and almost ran into the fire. "That ain't no Spaniard, Ben. That's a Confederate lieutenant. They're on our side!"

Ben grunted. From somewhere he produced a brass ship's lantern and lit it with a stick from the fire. He held it close, and in its yellow light they could see his face. His nose was hooked and rather large. There was a scar on one of his unshaven cheeks. Around his head was a dirty, red bandanna, and a single gold earring dangled from one ear. A crooked smile crossed his ancient, weathered face as he looked closely at the terrified Partridge.

"A strange little fish, this one is," Ben said, scratching his chin. "But if ye vouches for him, I'll take him across too. Got to wait for morning, though. Tide's running too fast now."

Partridge let out a sigh of relief as Ben jammed his cutlass into the ground by the fire and sat down. "I heard tell there was a war goin' on. An' now ye say it's coming here?" Ben asked.

"Yankees landed soldiers at Galveston on Christmas Eve. There's fixin' ta be a big battle there in a couple of days," Luke said.

At last Partridge spoke up. "That's — that's a military secret, Cochrane! You're not supposed to be telling anyone."

Ben looked squarely at Partridge and said, "It don't matter none, ye fool. There's always been somebody fightin' somebody in Texas. Old Ben's been fightin' so long he don't much care who no more.

"First, it was Indians. Kronks was always fightin' with all the other tribes — till the Spanish come. Spanish couldn't tell one Indian from another, so they just fought 'em all. Then there was the privateers like Lafitte and Aury and those like me what sailed with 'em. We fought

26

the Spanish and Indians and the English too, until the Americans come and run us out. Americans fought the Mexicans, and now ye tell me they be fighti͏ͅ them- selves. Don't make a lot of sense to me."

The fire had died to a bed of glowing embers. To the east was a bank of high clouds, glowing in the moonlight. As Luke drifted off to sleep, he could see Ben sitting close to the fire and staring off across the bay.

*   *   *   *

It was several hours after sunrise before the tide slacked enough for them to cross Clear Creek. Ben's boat was a sort of sailing barge, just big enough to carry one horse at a time, so three trips were required to carry both horses and riders across. Nevertheless, the sun was still low when the job was completed and they all stood on the north bank of the creek.

Ben looked at them strangely and smiled. "Ye re- minds me of a couple of lads who used to come this way many a year ago," he said. "Good luck to ya both, and take care."

"Thanks, Ben," Luke said, waving his hand as they rode off. "And Happy New Year!"

The trail wound deep into a swampy forest where cy- press trees towered ghostlike in the morning mist. Everywhere were ferns and palmetto bushes, wet and dripping with cold dew. Spanish moss hung like long cob- webs from the trees, and a carpet of decaying leaves and branches covered the ground.

"How much farther is it?" Partridge asked without bothering to look at his map.

"We can make it by tonight, easy," Luke answered and kept his horse moving.

"Are you sure that old man can be trusted?" Par- tridge asked again. He nervously looked back over his shoulder.

"I never knew Old Ben to hurt anyone who wasn't tryin' to hurt him."

Partridge sniffed. "He certainly does not look trustworthy to me."

Luke just shrugged and kept going. It seemed that the best way to get along with Partridge was to say nothing. He told himself that by nightfall they would be home. Then he could show Partridge the boat and be done with him. It would be lonely at the farm until his father returned, but there was work to do and he would keep busy. The time would pass faster that way.

In the early afternoon the trail wound down near a bayou. At one place it disappeared into the water and appeared again some fifty yards away on the other side. Luke reined his horse on the bank and watched the far bank for a while. Partridge halted beside him and immediately asked, "What are you waiting for?"

"Watchin' for gators," Luke said.

"Gators?"

"Yeah, alligators. There's a big one hangs around here sometimes. Been known to take a bite out of a horse now and then." As he spoke, they saw what had at first appeared to be a floating log turn slowly against the current and head toward them. "There he is now."

Partridge drew his army revolver. "I'll take care of him. No alligator is going to make me wait." Before Luke could protest, Partridge aimed over his horse's ears and fired. The pistol ball raised a little fountain of water ten yards from the alligator and, in the gray cloud of powder smoke which followed, the horse bolted into the bayou. Partridge toppled from the saddle and caught his foot in the stirrup as he fell.

Luke fought to control his own mount and then watched in horror as Partridge's horse splashed across the bayou, dragging the young lieutenant behind him. The alligator turned to follow but was easily outdistanced by the fleeing horse. Hitting the far bank at a dead run, both horse and lieutenant vanished into the trees.

Ignoring the cruising alligator, Luke spurred his

own horse into the bayou and gave chase. One hundred yards into the trees, the girth on Partridge's saddle finally broke. As Luke rode up, Partridge was lying on the trail, moaning and holding his leg.

"You all right?" Luke asked.

"My leg! I think it's broken," Partridge sobbed. Luke dismounted, drew his knife, and cut away the gray wool uniform pant leg while Partridge continued to wince with pain. The leg was already badly swollen and turning blue-black in color.

"I reckon you're probably right about it being broke," Luke sighed.

"It can't be. I've got to ride. I've got to give the instructions to the ships tomorrow."

"You can't ride," Luke told him.

"Then what am I going to do?"

Luke thought for a moment. "Well, first we'll fix up a splint on your leg. The nearest cabin is the Taylors' place on Middle Bayou. They'll bring their wagon back for you."

"That will take too long. I've got to get my message to the ships tomorrow," Partridge again protested.

"It'll take too long if I come back for you. Just tell me what I need to tell the ships. I can still make it in time."

Partridge shook his head. "I can't tell you a military secret."

"All right then. You got another idea?" Luke pressed. Partridge did not. For a long time he just stared dejectedly into the swamp. "Dang it, Partridge, make up your mind. I got a long way to go and not much time ta do it in."

Partridge did not answer, and Luke was getting mad. "Come on, dang it. My pa's on the *Neptune* and I'm gonna get those orders to 'em." He paused for a moment and then a smile began to spread across his face. "If you don't tell me, I might just ride off and forget all about where you are."

Partridge shot him a frightened look. "You wouldn't do that."

"Come nightfall, that gator is gonna get hungry. Why, he'll come crawling up this here trail, sniffin' around till he finds you and has you for his supper."

Luke had almost mounted his horse before Partridge finally agreed. "All right," he said weakly. "The attack is to be at 1:00 A.M. on New Year's morning. The signal will be one cannon shot."

Luke wilted with relief. "Thanks," he said as he swung out of the saddle and began making a splint. "Mr. Taylor's cabin's not too far from here. I'll send him back for ya."

When he had finished with the splint, he took another few precious minutes to find Partridge's pistol and return it to him before riding away. He spurred the horse into a gallop, leaving Partridge sitting against a tree, and was soon out of sight.

6

Long, Lonely Road

Luke dug his heels into the horse's flanks and rode hard. It was near supper time when he approached the Taylors' cabin. Seeing no sign of life, he halted at the front gate and called out, "Hello!" His voice echoed through the trees and was answered only by the distant call of a wild bird. He felt uneasy, as if something was wrong. Cautiously, he eased his horse through the gate. The cabin door hung half open and the Taylors' horse and wagon were nowhere to be seen.

He called out once more and then dismounted. The door creaked on its hinges as he pushed it open and looked inside. The cabin was empty except for a table and a bed. Everything else had been taken away.

"Reckon they heard the Yankees took Galveston and figured they might come here too," Luke said, thinking aloud. "Partridge! Now what am I goin' to do about him?" he wondered as he returned to the porch. He knew that if he took the time to go back, he might not get his message delivered to the fleet.

By the time he had reached his horse, he knew there was only one answer. The fleet was depending on him. There might be hundreds of lives lost if he did not deliver his message. He swung up into the saddle and galloped off to the north. He would go back for Partridge after he had delivered the message.

The Taylor cabin had been several miles out of his way, and darkness overtook him while he was still some distance from the farm. Carefully picking his way through the night, he chewed a piece of jerky as he rode and tried to watch the trail. Sometime before midnight, fog rolled in off the bay and became so thick that he could barely see his horse's ears in front of him. Reluctantly, he dismounted and unsaddled. The ground was too damp for a fire and so he spent the rest of the night huddled against a tree, trying to keep warm.

Dawn came slowly through the cold, wet fog. The tree trunks were black silhouettes which vanished into the gray somewhere above the horse's head. Luke shivered as he rolled up his blankets and tied them to the saddle.

For another hour he picked his way through the fog and then climbed a low hill which he knew was just west of the farm. The split-rail fence, which he had spent most of one summer helping to build, came into sight, and then the cabin and barn.

An eerie silence hung over the place. The only movement came from a few chickens scratching for breakfast in the dirt in front of the barn. Luke figured that meant the Yankees had not come here — at least not yet. He walked his horse into the barn, forked some hay into one of the stalls, unsaddled, and left the tired horse to eat.

He hurried to the cabin next and took down the Spanish musket that hung over the fireplace. The old flintlock had been around since long before he was born. Last summer he had hunted wild turkey with it, and it had misfired about as often as it had fired. Now it was

33

the only weapon around. Hung over its thick barrel was a powderhorn and shot pouch.

Luke carefully dumped a measure of gunpowder down the barrel and then took one of the lead balls out of the shot pouch. He wrapped it in a small piece of cloth and placed it in the barrel. His hands were shaking a little as he removed the ramrod from its place under the barrel and used it to ram the ball down the barrel as hard as he could. Finally, he opened the flashpan near the hammer, poured a little more powder into it, and closed it again. The musket was ready to fire.

Slinging the powderhorn and shot pouch over his shoulder, Luke took the musket and left the cabin. He moved quickly and quietly as he headed down toward the shore of Galveston Bay. The Cochrane family boat was a little skiff about twelve feet long. Luke and his father had used it for fishing and sometimes for gathering wild bird eggs from the islands out in the bay. Jake had built a small pier for it in a tiny cove. It occurred to Luke that he had not even looked at the boat for several months.

The skiff was nearly half-full of water now as Luke set his musket down and found the wooden bucket they kept on the pier for bailing out the boat. For several minutes he bailed, sloshing water out of the little boat until only a few inches remained in the bottom.

Although the fog still hung heavily over the water, Luke was sure that it had to be midmorning. "General said the fleet should be passin' Morgan's Point this morning. In the fog like this, I won't be able to see 'em from shore," Luke thought. "Reckon I gotta row out into the middle of the channel."

He set the oars into their locks and laid the musket on the seat beside him. Casting off the mooring lines, he started rowing. The land faded behind him and he rowed into the fog. When he at last shipped his oars, his arms hurt and he felt tired. He slumped back against the bow and let the boat drift until it suddenly occurred to him that his feet were wet.

Sitting up with a start, he looked at the water which had risen halfway to the seat. "Dang it!" he whispered and reached for the bailing bucket. "This here old boat is tryin' ta sink under me."

7

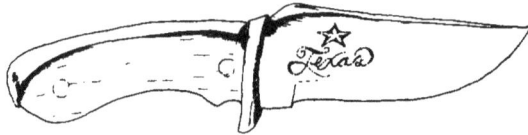

Sunk

Luke bailed until there was only an inch of water in the boat and then watched in horror as little fountains bubbled up between the planks. In a very short time, his feet were under water again.

Removing his coat and laying it on top of the musket, he bailed again until he was tired and sweating. All around him was fog — a wet, gray mist that hid both sky and water. There was not a breath of wind, and what little of the bay's surface that was visible looked like gray glass.

"Reckon I could row back to shore," Luke thought and then realized that he could no longer even tell in which direction the shore lay.

Another problem began to worry him. How was the fleet going to find him? The channel was narrow off Morgan's Point, but in this fog, he wondered if they would be able to see him at all. He bailed again and waited.

The hint of a breeze brushed his face and a few ripples stirred on the water. Somewhere, far in the distance, there seemed to be a rumbling — so quiet at first that he doubted it was real. Minutes slipped by. The rumbling grew slowly louder.

"Steamboat," he said aloud. "I sure hope they can see me." Luke rowed slowly in what he believed to be the direction from which the noise was coming. As it grew louder, it began to sound like two engines. He heard the churning of paddlewheels above the engine noise as a dark shadow took shape from out of the fog. "Hey!" he yelled, standing up in the boat and waving his hat. "I'm over here!"

Through the gray mist he could see a sidewheel steamer. It was the *Bayou City,* he was positive. But the ghostly silhouette showed no sign of changing course or even slowing down. Luke waved frantically, trying to attract the steamer's attention. So involved was he that he did not notice the long, curling bow wave which rushed at him through the mist. It lapped over the low sides of the little skiff and rocked it violently. Luke lost his balance and fell backward with his arms still waving.

Getting a mouthful of cold, salt water as his head went under, he choked and began to fight his way back to the surface. The first thing he saw when his head broke water was his little boat's bow, sinking beneath the bay. He felt for his knife and found it was still hanging on his belt. His hat floated a few feet away.

As he tried once more to wave at the fleeting shadow of the *Bayou City,* another shadow rose out of the fog. "The *Neptune!*" Luke thought. His father would be aboard her — so close and yet so impossible to reach. He waved as he tread water and yelled until his voice failed him. But the steamer continued on its slow, steady pace and vanished into the mist.

8

Fair Odds for Texans

Luke tried to catch his breath as he tread water. He would have to swim for shore, but which way? There were still little ripples across the water left from the *Neptune*'s wake. "Ships were headed south," he reasoned, "so the shore must be to my right." Unable to think of anything else to do, he struck out in the direction that he hoped the shore lay.

Almost at once, he heard another engine. Stopping for a moment and treading water, he listened. This engine sounded different, smaller perhaps. Out of the fog came a little steamboat, only about thirty feet long and moving very slowly. She was piled high with stacks of firewood, and men with rifles were sitting here and there on her deck. They were so close that Luke could clearly see their faces.

With failing strength, he waved his tired arms again. One of the men looked strangely at him for what seemed like a very long time and then suddenly pointed and started yelling. The little steamboat at once came to life as her paddlewheel went into reverse and her bow began to swing in Luke's direction. The dark hull eased up alongside him, and a big hand reached down to help him aboard.

"What ya doin' down there, boy?" a voice said, "Takin' a bath?"

Luke gasped for breath as he was hauled up over the side. "I got to get on the *Bayou City*! It's real important!"

"Is it now?" someone was asking suspiciously. "Just what's so important?"

Luke sat up, dripping bay water on the deck and shivering. "Got a message for Leon Smith," he said.

The man standing over him wore a captain's hat and was scratching his black beard. Around him were a dozen other men, all looking at Luke. "This sure don't look like no lieutenant I ever seen," one of them remarked.

"Lieutenant broke his fool leg," Luke told them, beginning to get angry. "I come in his place." Then he added sheepishly, " 'Cept my boat sunk."

There was a low murmur of laughter. The man in the captain's hat yelled over his shoulder, "Get some steam in this here tea kettle. We best be gettin' our young gentleman over to the flagship."

Someone put a blanket over Luke's shoulders as the little steamboat hurried off through the fog. "You're aboard the *Lucy Gwin*," the man in the captain's hat said. "We're hauling wood to refuel the *Bayou City* before the fight starts. She's up ahead just a bit."

Luke nodded and shivered as the minutes dragged by. "Steamer off the weather bow," the lookout called. "Looks to be the *Bayou City*." A few more long, cold minutes passed before the two steamers eased alongside each other with only a gentle bump. A friendly hand grabbed Luke as he jumped across the narrow strip of water separating them.

On board the *Bayou City*, Luke was hurried into one of the big cabins where Captain Smith was waiting for

39

him. Smith was a big man with a goatee and wild, blue eyes which bore through Luke like the cold, north wind. He wore a gray naval officer's coat, and two big Dance Brothers revolvers were stuck in his belt. He looked down at the wet boy for a long moment before he spoke. "Where did you come from?" he asked finally.

"I — I brung a message from General Magruder, sir. He says he's gonna start attackin' the Yankees at one o'clock tomorrow morning."

Smith grunted. "And he sent you out here to tell me that?"

"Well . . . no, sir. He sent Lieutenant Partridge. I was just supposed to show him where my pa's boat was so he could row out with the message. But the lieutenant broke his leg, and I had to leave him in the swamp. Ya got to send somebody back for him."

A long silence followed as Smith nodded his head several times. "You did good, lad. We thank you. But I can't spare anyone to go back for Partridge until this battle is over. Fact is, I can't even spare anyone to get you ashore. This Lieutenant Partridge will just have to make it on his own until then. Now, you better go below and get dried out a bit."

Luke felt relieved that he had done the right thing by leaving Partridge in the swamp. "Sir," he ventured, "my pa's Jake Cochrane. He's gunner on the *Neptune*. I'd like to get over there if I could."

Smith nodded again. "So you're Jake's boy. I should have known. You do favor him a bit." Smith turned to an officer beside him and ordered, "Signal *Lucy Gwin* to come alongside." The officer left and Smith turned back to Luke. "They'll take you across. We'll be reducing speed shortly so we don't get too close to the Yankee fleet before nightfall."

"Thank you, sir," Luke said. On a sudden impulse he added, "You know my pa?"

Smith laughed. "Mostly by his reputation. He was pretty famous once, you know."

40

Luke did not know but decided not to ask any more questions.

Lucy Gwin came alongside and Luke jumped aboard. In a few minutes he was again standing on the old *Neptune,* facing his father.

"Boy, I told you to stay ashore," Jake greeted him gruffly. "What do you think you're doin' out here?"

"I'm sorry, Pa, but I couldn't help it. First that dang fool lieutenant broke his leg, and then the boat sunk under me, and the *Lucy Gwin* fished me outa the bay, and I just had to get the message to Captain Smith and — aw heck, Pa, I didn't know how else to do it."

Jake shook his head. "Dang it. The last thing I want is you on this boat when the shootin' starts." He looked up at the hurricane deck and then added, "Come on."

"Sangster!" Jake blurted out as he burst into the pilothouse, "You gotta find a place to put my boy ashore. This wasn't in our deal."

Sangster took the outburst calmly and scratched his beard. "Don't know where that'd be, Jake. I'd go aground for sure in this fog. Only good channel is into Clear Creek, and that's seven miles west. Can't do that. I'd lose contact with the fleet and we'd never catch up."

"Come on, Bill. There's got to be some way."

"I could drop him on Red Fish Island. Some passin' boat might pick him up."

Jake shook his head. "Heck, if we don't win this fool battle, there ain't gonna be no passin' boats."

"I want to stay, Pa," Luke interrupted suddenly.

"No." His father's voice was ice cold.

Sangster's next words were quietly spoken. "How old was you, Jake, when you was powder monkey on the *Swift,* privateering against the Mexicans?"

"Too danged young to have a lick of sense."

"I reckon you was about twelve," Sangster said. "I remember 'cause I was a gunner's mate. Seems like I was about fifteen then."

"That was all different," Jake defended.

"Only difference I can see is that your pa weren't around to say no."

Jake slammed his fist onto the chart table. "Tarnation, ain't there no other way?"

"I don't see one, Jake. The *Lucy Gwin* and the *Carr* are loaded to their gunnels with cord wood and fixin' to refuel us after dark, so I can't send him ashore with one of them. And Smith ain't about to let me take a chance of the *Neptune* goin' aground somewhere."

Jake turned away with a curse and stared blankly out of the windows. Luke moved beside him and tugged gently on his sleeve. "I'm sorry, Pa. But I promise I'll be real careful. Besides, it's been just you an' me since Ma died. I reckon maybe we're just supposed to do this thing together."

Jake gave him no answer but continued to stare out across the gray waters of Galveston Bay. The fog was lifting. There was the slightest hint of sunshine. Ahead they could see the *Bayou City,* her huge sidewheels churning up white water as she plowed south. Running beside her were the little steamers *Lucy Gwin* and *John Carr.*

"Some fleet," Jake said bitterly. "Three field cannon and less than three hundred men on two rotten old bay steamers, and a couple of launches that got no business outside the harbor. Somewhere out there, near as we can figure, there's six Yankee gunboats mounting a total of over thirty guns, and maybe three companies of marines thrown in for good measure."

" 'Bout fair odds for Texans," Sangster said.

42

9

Eve of Battle

The last gray wisps of fog had vanished and the sun was just setting in the west as Jake swung down the rusty iron steps which led to the *Neptune*'s foredeck. Luke was hurrying behind him. Jake crossed to where the two cannon were lashed in place. "Move them canister rounds back by the hatch," he ordered the closest man. "If they get wet, we'll be stuck with a barrel full of oversized buck shot and no way to get it out."

The man picked up one of the short, metal cylinders with a paper bag nailed to one end. Wanting to help, Luke reached for the other end, but his father grabbed his collar. "First rule around here," Jake said crossly. "You don't have no part in this battle. You don't do nothin' but stay out of the way."

Luke was shocked. For as long as he could remember, he had always been expected to help out and share in the work, no matter what it was. "Why, Pa?" he asked.

" 'Cause I said so. This ain't no Sunday social. Look

43

around you, son. A bunch of these men you see are gonna be dead by this time tomorrow. When the shootin' starts, you're goin' below, and you're gonna stay there no matter what happens. Is that clear?"

"Yes, sir," Luke answered solemnly. "I know that, but I just wanted to help."

For a second, Jake's hard frown softened, and then he turned away. "Just stay out of the way," he added.

Luke sat down on a cotton bale. He felt hurt that his father was unhappy about his being there. The excitement of the coming battle was intoxicating, and thoughts of death had been far from his mind.

He left the deck and wandered into the saloon where the extra powder and shot were stored. There a thin young man was stacking powder bags against the wall. His sandy hair looked as if it had been cut by placing a bowl over his head and cutting around it. Luke guessed that he was not much older than himself.

"Howdy," Luke said.

"Howdy, yourself," the young man returned. "You're Jake's boy, ain't you?"

"Yeah. What ya doin'?"

"Getting these here rounds ready for the fight. My name's Andy, but they just call me the 'powder monkey.' "

"Powder monkey?" Luke frowned. "That sounds silly."

Andy nodded and kept working. "Reckon it does. But that's what they call the boy who keeps the cannons supplied with powder. You can't keep much powder just layin' around on deck during a battle, 'cause it might catch fire and explode. So they store it somewhere back out of the way and then carry just enough to the guns each time they fire."

Luke pondered the statement. "You ever been in a battle before?"

Andy stopped what he was doing and looked up. "Not on no boat, I ain't. I was with Sibley in New Mexico, but that was different — had good solid ground under my feet then. All you had to worry about was gettin' shot. Out here, you might get drowned too."

As the hours dragged by, Luke could do nothing except try to stay out of the way of the hurried activities as, all around him, the men prepared for battle. More ropes were brought out to tie down the cotton bales. Powder and shot were distributed to the soldiers as they cleaned their rifles. Down in the engine room, a grinding wheel turned constantly, sharpening cutlasses and sabers. Everyone seemed to be in a hurry — everyone, that is, except Luke.

The western shore of Edwards Point was barely visible against the night sky as the fleet threaded its way through the narrow channel between the low, sandy islands called Red Fish Bar. A hot meal of beans and tough beef was passed around. A silence hung over the *Neptune*'s decks as the soldiers ate. Each man seemed to be lost in his own private thoughts and fears.

Luke found his father sitting against one of the cotton bales beside the cannons. They sat together in silence as somewhere a harmonica played the sad notes of an old song from more peaceful times.

"You ought to get some sleep," Jake said at last.

"Don't reckon I could. I'm too excited," Luke answered. "Tell me about the Battle of Campeche."

"What?" Jake's voice was distant.

"You know. Captain Sangster said you shot the flagstaff off the *Guadalupe*."

Jake took a deep breath and stared into the night. "It was back before Texas was part of the United States — about '43, near as I can remember. Anyhow, the Mexican navy was pretty big then, and they were fighting a rebellion down on the Yucatan. Word was that they were planning to take Texas next, so Commodore Moore took the Texas navy down to help the revolutionaries.

"Sangster and me was on a sloop-of-war named the *Austin*. The Mexicans had some steamers then, but the

45

Texas navy was all sailing ships. So we had to wait for the wind before we could attack. And that year the wind just didn't cooperate at all. Every time we'd try to get close, the Mexican steamers would just back off, up into the wind where we couldn't follow.

"But anyhow, we finally got a little breeze and sailed in close enough for our guns to do some damage. The *Guadalupe* was the Mexican admiral's ship. We shot her flagstaff off and damaged one of her paddlewheels so she couldn't move away. 'Course, by then, she'd done us a fair amount of damage in return. Her big guns were firing Paixhans shells."

"What are those?" Luke asked.

"Well, each one weighs sixty-eight pounds and they explode when they hit. The *Austin* took nine hits in twenty minutes. But we still chased 'em off, and history says we won. Leastways, Mexico hasn't tried to invade Texas again."

The *Neptune* had stopped her engine and was barely drifting forward through the night. "Where are we?" Luke asked.

Jake pointed to a dark shadow of land off the starboard bow. "Over there's Pelican Island. Those lights beyond it are Galveston."

An excited voice pierced the night. "Steamer off the port bow!" All eyes turned in that direction. Against the night sky was the long, low silhouette of a sidewheel steamer, lying silently and showing no lights.

Luke's father brushed past him in a hurry. "Load!" he ordered his men in a loud whisper.

46

10

False Start

The only sounds were the hiss of steam escaping from the *Neptune*'s leaky boiler and the steady splashing of water being pumped over her side. Fifty yards off the starboard side, the *Bayou City* was a dark outline — unmoving, but poised to strike. The steamer which lay across the bow was also stopped and silent.

Beside him in the dark, Luke could hear the charges being "rammed home" as Jake directed the loading of the twenty-four-pounders. "Range . . . five hundred yards," he was saying in a calm voice.

Soldiers hurried forward, thrusting their rifles across the tops of the cotton bales. Rifles were cocked with a steady stream of clicks which echoed in the night like an unsteady clock.

"Looks like the Yankee flagship *Westfield*," Sangster said from the deck above. "Hold your fire, men. We're going to try to back away before she spots us."

The *Neptune*'s paddlewheels began to turn slowly in

reverse. Alongside her, it was clear that the *Bayou City* was doing the same thing. "Why ain't we gonna fight 'em, Pa?" Luke asked.

"It's too early. If we go shootin' now, it will just let the Yankees know there's fixin' to be an attack. We don't even want to be seen before that signal gun goes off."

Even as he spoke, there was a bright flash from the *Westfield*. A split second later, thunder rolled across the water, followed by the terrifying scream of an incoming round.

Cold terror froze Luke where he stood. He felt as though that one huge cannonball was flying directly at his nose and there was nothing he could do to stop it or even get out of the way. A hand grabbed him and pulled him down behind a cotton bale just as a fountain of water rose between the two steamers. "Get your head down, boy," Jake was telling him. "Can't you see we're gettin' shot at?"

Luke only nodded. He was too scared to speak.

A single rifle cracked from somewhere aboard the *Neptune* and Sangster's voice boomed down from the hurricane deck, "Confound it, ya landlubbers! I said hold your fire. That Yankee don't know what he's shootin' at!" The *Neptune*'s paddlewheel began to turn faster. The *Bayou City* kept up the pace beside her, and the two smaller steamers were somewhere safely astern.

The Yankee ship chose not to follow and faded back into the darkness. Perhaps, as Sangster had said, they only thought they saw something and, knowing they had no friends in this part of the bay, fired just to see if the enemy would shoot back. Or perhaps the *Westfield* suspected a trap. Aboard the *Neptune,* they could only guess.

The little fleet retreated until they sounded the shallow water around Halfmoon Shoal, and then lay quietly, waiting for the signal to go into battle.

One o'clock and then two o'clock passed. The signal gun had still not been fired. Sangster was pacing the hurricane deck and chewing on his pipe. Everyone else just

48

sat quietly. Luke found that he was shaking all over. He pulled an old army blanket tighter around his shoulders and poked his hands deep into his pockets, but it did no good. It was fear, not the cold night air, which was making him shiver. Never had he known fear like this — a fear so overpowering that it took total control of him and left him unable to think or move. He stood for a long time with his face pressed against a cotton bale.

Sometime later, Jake put a hand on his shoulder. "You all right, son?"

Luke nodded as tears filled his eyes. "Aw, dang it all, Pa, I got all scared and the battle ain't even started yet."

Jake almost laughed and, for a moment, Luke felt even worse. "That's good, son," Jake said, " 'cause if you weren't scared, then I'd know something was bad wrong with you."

Luke looked up and wiped away his tear. "Huh?"

"Out here, the only folks that aren't scared near to death are either crazy or just plain stupid. Now, some men hide it a little better than others, but there ain't a livin' soul in this whole fleet who ain't wishin' he was someplace else. And you can be sure that once the shootin' really starts, everyone of us, myself included, is gonna be wishin' our mamas had never met our papas."

"You mean you're scared too, Pa?"

Jake huffed quietly. "You danged right I'm scared."

"But you been in battle before."

"That don't help much. Fact is, sometimes I think it makes it worse, 'cause you can remember how bad it was last time."

Luke looked away and felt terrible.

"If it's any comfort, I reckon the worst part is right now, when there's nothin' to do but sit and wait for it to start."

Far away there was a single, dull explosion. Several seconds later, the distant popping of rifle fire drifted over the water. The *Bayou City*'s paddlewheels suddenly began to turn, churning up a cauldron of white water

49

which glowed in the darkness as the steamer lunged forward.

From the *Neptune*'s hurricane deck, they could all hear Sangster yelling: "Full ahead! Get this dang-blasted rust bucket moving!"

A blood-curdling "rebel yell" went up from the fleet as the steamers began to move forward. At long last, it was beginning.

11

First Blood

Dawn displayed many shades of pastel pink and purple. Seconds before the sun peeked over the eastern horizon, the blood-red battle flags of the Confederacy soared up the flagstaffs on the *Bayou City* and the *Neptune*. They caught the first golden rays of sunrise and shone like blazing flares between the smokestacks.

The *Bayou City* was a hundred yards ahead and lengthening the distance with every turn of her paddlewheel. The *Neptune*'s rotten deck planks vibrated, and white water boiled around her bow. A red glow from her fireboxes reflected from the open engine room hatchway. Steam hissed from below.

Even from his position inside the saloon, Luke could hear Sangster cursing both engine and engineer for not giving him more speed. "Tie down the blasted safety valves, ya lily-livered baboon! And give me more steam, or I'll feed *you* into them boilers!"

"Steamers off the bow!" came a cry from atop the pilothouse. Sangster charged out onto the hurricane deck with a telescope in his hand. All eyes were on him as he focused the glass first to port and then to starboard.

"That's the *Westfield* to port and the *Harriet Lane* to starboard," he announced. "*Westfield* will try to cut us off, so we'll turn and draw his fire. Try to give *Bayou City* time to close with the *Lane!*"

The *Neptune's* bow swung slowly around until the *Westfield* was dead ahead. "Mr. Cochrane!" Sangster bellowed again. "You may fire when ready."

Luke ran to the forward saloon windows. Although cotton bales had been piled in front of them, he could still see a little of the forward deck. His father was crouched behind one of the guns, with the lanyard in his hand as he sighted over the barrel. Suddenly, he stepped aside and said, "Well, here goes for a New Year's present."

The discharge rattled the window frames and smoke rolled back over the *Neptune's* deck. A little fountain of water rose close to the *Westfield's* bow.

"On line and short," Sangster called down the correction.

As the gun crew worked feverishly to reload, Jake stepped to the other twenty-four-pounder and adjusted the range. "Fire!" he called, stepping away from the gun's recoil. This time, a cheer went up from the *Neptune* as the shot glanced off the Yankee's hull and skipped away over the water. At almost the same instant, the *Westfield* began returning fire. One shell exploded in the water, close along the starboard beam. Another missed the stern by only a few yards.

Luke squinted to get a look at the charging enemy. She was a sidewheeler, bigger than anything he had seen before. Guns bristled from her sides and bow like a monstrous porcupine.

Another round whined high over the *Neptune's* pilothouse and Luke ducked instinctively. Then, both of the *Neptune's* twenty-four-pounders fired almost at the same time. Again, a cheer went up as both shells found their mark.

Suddenly, the *Neptune* was turning away, back toward the *Bayou City*. Andy ran into the saloon and grabbed up two more powder bags. Smoke had blackened him from head to foot, and sweat had left ugly streaks down his grimy face.

"What's goin' on?" Luke blurted out, desperate for information. "Why are we turnin' back?"

Andy talked as he picked up the charges. "Our shells ain't doin' no damage to him. Sangster's gonna try to run him aground!" Without stopping, Andy hurried to the door. Luke was starting to ask him something else when there was a flash of light, a hundred times brighter than lightning. Something picked Luke up and threw him against the floor.

His ears rang and when he forced his eyes open, smoke hung thick and heavy in the saloon. Andy was lying in the doorway. His blackened shirt was now stained with red.

"Andy!" Luke stammered as he painfully rose to his feet and started toward him. Andy did not answer; his eyes stared sightlessly up at the ceiling. Beyond the doorway, a gray-clad soldier lay on the deck and at least two cotton bales had vanished completely, along with several feet of railing. Luke felt himself shaking again as he knelt beside Andy. Although he could not have explained it, he knew that the powder monkey was dead.

He wanted to hide somewhere, to crawl into the deepest hole he could find and not come out, or even think, until the battle was over.

Somewhere — it seemed far away — his father was calling. Moments passed before he realized that he was calling for more powder. The powder bags were still there, piled against the wall, and they did not appear damaged. But to take them out to the guns meant going out on deck — going out there where men were dying; going out into that holocaust which had just killed Andy.

Again, Jake's voice echoed inside Luke's head. "Powder up! Bring up those charges!"

Luke moved at last. He started for the pile of powder bags, tripped over Andy's body, and fell flat on his face, but he never slowed down. Still on his hands and knees, he grabbed two charges and was surprised how heavy they were.

A shell screamed overhead and exploded in the distance as he raced out onto the deck with a charge under each arm. Dodging the dead soldier's body, he ran for the guns.

Jake saw him coming, and the world stopped for a moment as they faced each other. Luke, small and already grimy from the smoke, stood with a heavy powder bag under each arm. Jake, also blackened from the first exchange of fire and bleeding from a cut on his forehead, towered above him. There was a look in his eyes that Luke had seen only a few times before: once, when Luke had killed a wild turkey just as it took flight, and again when he had driven the team and wagon without running into anything for the first time. One day, years later, he would realize that it was something called "respect."

"Andy's dead," Luke said evenly. "I'll take his place."

Jake nodded and took the charges. "Keep 'em comin'," he said.

12

Moment of Truth

Captain Sangster was acting like an excited child at Christmas. His laughter was almost hysterical as he jumped up and down on the hurricane deck with his telescope in one hand. A Paixhans shell had just exploded harmlessly over the water. "Dang Yankee skipper done run his ignorant self aground on Pelican Spit!" he announced as he pointed at the *Westfield*.

A cheer went up through the *Neptune* and echoed above the other sounds of battle. But the celebration was short-lived. Far ahead, the *Bayou City* shuddered as an explosion wreaked havoc on her foredeck. Cotton bales and whole sections of deck railing flew off into the water as if slapped at by some giant hand.

Sangster's silly grin vanished as he focused his telescope in that direction. "Looks like her gun blew up!" he said, lowering the telescope. "But Smith is gonna try to get alongside the *Lane* anyway. If we can't get there to help, he ain't got much of a chance."

Jake was already cranking up the elevation wheels on the two twenty-four-pounders when Sangster began cursing the engineer for more speed. Within seconds, the *Neptune* had turned, and the long, rakish outline of the *Harriet Lane* was squarely off the bow. "Fire!" Jake ordered, and both guns discharged in unison, clouding the deck with smoke and shaking the whole ship with their recoil.

Sangster's telescope went to his eye as the *Lane* appeared framed in a rolling bank of gunsmoke. "Ya hit 'em Jake, my boy. Now, just keep it up."

A shell exploded near the *Neptune*'s bow, sending a cold spray of seawater across the foredeck and drenching the guns and gunners. "Well, that means she knows we're here. Now she's got two targets to worry about," Jake said.

Again and again, Jake's twenty-four-pounders found their mark. Through his telescope, Sangster counted several neat, round holes in the *Lane*'s hull, but she continued to return fire as if nothing was wrong.

The *Neptune* charged in like an old racehorse, desperate to win this one last race. The deck rattled beneath their feet, and even the smokestacks shook violently as the boat's overworked engine tried to tear away from its iron mounts. When Luke again had time to look up, he was surprised to see that the *Bayou City* was only about one hundred yards ahead.

The *Lane*'s bow began to swing away as the *Bayou City* closed the last two hundred yards. "Smith has gotten in too close for the *Lane*'s bow guns to bear," Jake panted, without looking up from his priming, "so she's trying to run off and keep some sea room between them."

The *Neptune*'s crew watched spellbound as the *Bayou City* closed the last few yards. The *Lane* was backing her paddlewheels when the *Bayou City* rammed into her long bowsprit. A hail of rifle fire erupted from both ships as they hung, locked together, for a few desperate moments. The gangplanks on *Bayou City*'s bow were

dropped but did not reach far enough for her crew to board the *Lane*. Then the two ships slowly began to drift apart.

"They're done for now," someone cried. "*Bayou City* must have jammed her steering in the collision."

The disabled steamer drifted farther and farther away. The *Lane* began to swing also, turning slowly to bring the nine-inch cannons of her broadside to bear against the disabled *Bayou City*.

Sangster was gripping the deck rail with white knuckles. "It ain't over yet!" He cursed and then called a calm order to the guns, "Mr. Cochrane . . . Grapeshot, double-charged if you please."

"Aye, aye, sir!" Jake returned sharply in a voice so charged with excitement that Luke barely recognized that it was his father speaking. Without waiting for instructions or allowing himself time to think about the implications, he ran for the saloon to bring up the powder charges. When he returned to the foredeck, the *Lane* had grown to an immense size and loomed dark and deadly off the bow. The air was alive with rifle balls and flying splinters, which buzzed and screamed like so many angry hornets.

A gunner's mate lay wounded beside the starboard gun, his leg bleeding onto the deck. A soldier fell in front of Luke, but Luke jumped neatly over the body without even slowing down. Sour-smelling smoke choked him and burned his eyes as he handed the powder bags to his father. In a few seconds, the guns were loaded and Jake was attaching the lanyards and friction tubes.

One of the *Neptune*'s smokestacks toppled in a cloud of smoke and soot as the *Lane*'s parrot rifle fired a little high. Bits of rusty metal rained down on the decks, but Sangster ignored the damage as a down draft sent black smoke curling around him. Another gunner's mate dropped suddenly as he crouched behind the guns. Luke could clearly see the men aboard the *Lane* now. Their heads, shoulders, and rifles were just visible above the bulwarks as they fired desperately at the charging *Neptune*.

"Shoot, Pa! Hurry up before we hit!" Luke heard himself shout at the top of his lungs.

"Not just yet," Jake answered, his voice calm and concentrating. The *Lane's* spray-drenched hull loomed ever larger as they closed the last fifty yards. Luke saw an officer jump on top of one of the *Lane's* paddlewheel housings and aim his pistol at them. The first shot whined off the gun carriage beside them. Then Luke saw his father jerk backward and slump against the wheel.

"I'm hit," Jake said calmly.

"Pa!" Luke yelled and moved beside him as an ugly red stain spread over his shoulder. Another pistol ball slammed into the gun carriage, inches from Luke's ear. His eyes fell on the revolver in his father's belt, and he reached for it. The big Navy Colt was heavy, and he needed both hands to raise it. Time seemed to move at a snail's pace as he cocked the hammer and swung the sights toward the figure on the *Lane's* paddle box. Without realizing he had pulled the trigger, Luke saw the hammer drop, saw the cap spark, and the pistol raise up in his hands. Smoke whipped back across his face, and when he could see again, the officer was falling into the gap of tossing water between the two ships.

Jake lifted the pistol from his trembling hands. "I can't pull both of these lanyards," he said and winced in pain. "You'll have to help me."

Luke nodded, still in a daze.

"When I tell you, pull on this real hard."

Tears were clouding his vision as Luke gripped the length of heavy cord. The *Lane* was so close that he could almost count the nails in her hull. Time seemed to stand still, to crystallize and refuse to move forward. It seemed that every rifle on the *Lane* was aimed exactly between his eyes. At any second he would be blown into little pieces and scattered across the restless waters of Galveston Bay.

"Now, son . . . fire!"

13

Boarders Away

Luke jerked on the lanyard with all his might. There was a slight hiss of powder igniting, and then the gun raised up off the deck, bellowing out a roar which deafened him to all but the ringing somewhere inside his head. Hot air blasted across his face. The *Harriet Lane* disappeared behind the cloud of rolling powder smoke. When she appeared again, a whole section of her bulwark was gone, leaving only the jagged ends of timbers and twisted iron. Her deck was littered with fallen rigging and bodies.

"Get outa here. We're gonna ram her!" Jake was yelling as Luke felt himself being lifted by the collar. His legs were already churning like *Neptune*'s paddlewheel before he hit the deck. Jake and Luke were running for the cover of the cotton bales stacked against the saloon wall when the sound of splintering wood reached their ears. The deck buckled beneath them. Luke threw himself forward, over the cotton bales, and landed hard amid a shower of falling rigging and timbers.

When he dared to look back, he saw that the *Neptune*'s foredeck was a wreck. The old steamer had driven into the *Lane* just forward of her port side paddlewheel. Deck planks were broken and splintered, and the entire bow was sticking up at an odd angle. Cotton bales were scattered about, and one of the twenty-four-pounders lay on its side. The other cannon sat with its muzzle against the splintered deck and one of the carriage wheels broken at the hub.

The two gangplanks, which were supposed to drop forward and allow soldiers to rush aboard the enemy vessel, were now broken and hanging in a tangled mess of the *Lane*'s rigging. Steam was hissing in white clouds from the engine room hatchway and between cracks in the deck.

"Get to Sangster," Jake gasped. "Tell him the steam pipes are ruptured and we're sinkin'!"

"What about your arm?" Luke insisted.

"It ain't bad. Now get goin'."

Luke sprinted up the stairs to the hurricane deck. The railing was lined with riflemen now, firing and loading as fast as they could. "That's the way, boys," Sangster's voice boomed above the shooting. "Keep 'em duckin'."

Luke dodged through the crowd and found Sangster in the pilothouse. Grabbing at the sleeve of his coat, he yelled, "Pa says the steam pipes are busted and we're sinkin'!"

Sangster nodded. "Figured as much, dang blast it all. Worse yet, the gangplanks is all fouled up so we can't board her." They both ducked as rifle fire shattered several windows, sending slivers of broken glass flying everywhere.

Confusion ruled aboard the *Harriet Lane* too. Most of

61

the gun crews were huddled behind the deck house. Time and again, they watched their shipmates attempt to man the huge cannons of the *Lane*'s main battery. Each time they tried, rifle fire from the *Neptune* drove them back. But now the *Lane*'s detachment of marines were beginning to concentrate their fire, and the *Neptune*'s pilothouse looked like Swiss cheese.

"Captain, look!" someone was shouting at Sangster. "*Bayou City*'s got her steering fixed and she's coming back!"

Luke peeked up from behind the pilothouse bulkhead. Beyond the battle which raged between the *Neptune* and the *Harriet Lane,* he could see the *Bayou City.* White water churned around her paddlewheels and smoke billowed from her smokestacks. Soldiers were crowded on her bow, and she was charging in toward the *Lane*'s unprotected starboard side. Before the *Lane*'s crew realized what was happening, *Bayou City* was alongside and a gray wave of boarders, led by cutlass-wielding Leon Smith, had swarmed over her side. Her decks disappeared beneath a fog of powder smoke until only smokestacks were visible above the battle. The Union flag, flying from the *Lane*'s masthead, fluttered slowly down and vanished in the smoke.

"Cease fire!" Sangster ordered. "She's struck her colors. It's over. They surrender!"

The sudden silence was as deafening as the battle had been before it. Luke could hear the hiss of steam and the gurgling of water around the *Neptune*'s hull. Somewhere, sea gulls were crying. He squinted his eyes and realized that the sun was shining. It was a beautiful day.

To the east, four other ships — the entire blockading fleet — were also striking their colors and surrendering.

Jake appeared at the pilothouse door with a crude bandage around his arm. Sangster turned and smiled broadly, extending his big hand. "Congratulations, Jake.

You're as fine a gunner today as you were twenty years ago. Maybe better."

Jake only smiled back and nodded.

With the last ounces of steam from her leaking boilers, the *Neptune* backed away from the *Lane* and limped in slowly toward the Galveston shore. She finally grounded on the mud flats near the end of 32nd street. Seawater drowned her fires, and she settled onto the mud with her main deck still a few inches above the water.

Five minutes later, the Union flagship *Westfield*, still hard aground on Pelican Spit, exploded in a ball of flame, and wreckage began to drop into the water hundreds of yards away. The remaining three Union ships quickly ran for the open sea. With the *Neptune* out of action and the *Bayou City* badly damaged, the Confederates had nothing with which to chase them.

Ashore, the firing had also stopped as the small remaining Union land force saw their navy abandon them. They surrendered immediately. The Bonny Blue Flag of the Confederacy was once again hoisted above Galveston.

Luke and Jake were rowed ashore later that day. They landed at Kuhn's Wharf, at 18th Street, where most of the land fighting had taken place. The first thing they saw as they climbed onto the dock was a skinny lieutenant on crutches and with a bandaged leg.

"Cochrane!" the officer called out and waved one hand as he hobbled toward them. "I wondered if you made it." The lieutenant's face sobered when he looked closely at Luke and his father. Their faces were blackened with smoke and grime and their eyes were red. They were both so tired that they could hardly stand. Luke's shirt was torn, and Jake's arm was in a sling. The Navy Colt revolver was stuck in Jake's belt. Luke's knife was at his side.

"Partridge," Luke exclaimed, uncertain why he was so happy to see his former companion. "I wondered if you made it too. How'd you get here so quick?"

Partridge's face was all smiles. Luke thought he looked a little older than he had just two days ago. Partridge thought the same thing about Luke. "Old Ben found me and took me back as far as the railroad tracks. I caught one of the supply trains last night."

"Great," Luke smiled back. "Looks like Galveston is all yours. Try not to lose it again."

Epilogue

The Confederate army did not lose Galveston again, although the war would drag on for two more long, hard years. The Union navy reinforced its blockade offshore but was never able to completely shut down shipping along the Texas coast.

The *Neptune* and the *Bayou City* would sail again in more peaceful times. Both were repaired, and Galveston long remembered them as the gallant ships they were.

The *Harriet Lane* finished the war flying the Confederate flag and was returned to the U.S. Revenue Service in 1865.

Commander Renshaw, commodore of the Union fleet, had ordered his flagship *Westfield* blown up to prevent its capture. He and twelve others were killed when the explosive charges they had set in the ship's powder magazine went off prematurely. The wreck of the *Westfield* lay for many years off the east end of Pelican Island, near where Seawolf Park stands today. Eventually, she disappeared during a hurricane. Today, most historians believe that her wreck is sunk in shallow water, just off the Pelican Island fishing pier.

The Confederate land and sea forces under General Magruder lost 143 men, killed and wounded. In addition to the two gunboats, the Union losses totaled about 600 men, including captives. The desperate venture had paid off.

Glossary

admiral: a high-ranking naval officer, usually in charge of a fleet of ships.

Allen's Landing: Located on Buffalo Bayou, at the end of Main Street, in Houston, Texas. During the Civil War, it was a landing for steamboats and other bay traffic.

Aury: Louis de Aury was a French privateer who established a settlement on Galveston Island in 1816. The following year, he was forced out by Jean Lafitte.

bail: to pump or dip water out of a boat.

battery: a military unit made up of usually between four and six cannons, and the men needed to move and fire them; also, the cannons located along one side of a warship.

bedroll: in Civil War times, this usually was nothing more than a rolled-up blanket and possibly a piece of canvas to keep off rain and dew.

bow wave: a sometimes dangerous wave, created by a ship's bow as it moves through the water.

bowsprit: a long, tapered spar extending in front of a ship's bow.

bulwark: the part of a ship's side which is above the deck.

carriage way: old term for street.

Confederate: the league of southern states during the American Civil War.

conscripted: drafted, forced into military service.

Dance Brothers revolvers: a brand of military revolvers built in Texas throughout the Civil War.

Edwards Point: point of land on west shore of Galveston Bay, now known as Eagle Point.

Federals: troops of the Federal government of the United States; Union soldiers.

firebox: the part of a steam engine where wood or coal is burned to heat water, which in turn creates steam.

flagship: the ship which carries the admiral, commodore, and other officer in command of a fleet of ships.

flashpan: the part of a flintlock weapon where the gunpowder is ignited by sparks from the flint.

flintlock: a muzzle-loading firearm which uses a piece of flint on the hammer to strike sparks which ignite the gunpowder.

foredeck: on a ship, the deck closest to the bow.

frigate: usually a medium-sized, fast warship with only one gun deck.

gangplank: a long wooden ramp, used to board a ship.

grapeshot: a cluster of small iron balls, fired from a cannon.

gunboat: a small armed ship, usually used for patrol and guard duty.

gunner's mates: sailors assigned to work on gun crews aboard a warship.

gunnery: the science of making and using heavy artillery.

Halfmoon Shoal: Formerly, a crescent-shaped oyster bar in Galveston Bay. Today, it is much smaller and located just north of the Texas City Dike.

hardtack: a hard, saltless bread formerly used as a military ration.

Harrisburg: During the Civil War, Harrisburg was located on Buffalo Bayou, near present-day Turning Basin. It later became part of Houston.

headquarters: the center of operations of a military command.

hilt: part of the handle of a sword or knife.

hurricane deck: the top, or highest, deck on a steamboat.

jimmyjohn: a jug with a round handle.

Kronks: slang for Carancahua, a tribe of cannibalistic Indians who once lived along the Texas coast.

launch: a small, open steamboat.

lieutenant: the lowest-ranking commissioned officer in the army.

marines: soldiers especially trained to fight aboard ships.

martial law: temporary rule issued by the army over civilians during time of war.

master gunner: the senior gunner, or gun captain, aboard a warship who would usually be in charge of gunnery training.

McClellen saddle: a type of military saddle used by the U.S. and Confederate cavalry during the Civil War and later.

Morgan's Point: a point of land and a community located on the northwestern shore of Galveston Bay.

musket: A single-shot, smooth-bore weapon fired from the shoulder. It is less accurate than a rifle because it does not have grooves in the barrel which cause the bullet to spin.

Paixhans shells: Exploding artillery shells, developed by French General Henri Paixhans (1783–1854).

parrot rifle: a type of rifled cannon capable of firing accurately at long ranges.

Pelican Island: an island in Galveston Bay, located just north of Galveston Island.

Pelican Spit: At the time of the Civil War, Pelican Spit was a small island, located close to Pelican Island. Fill was later added to make it part of present-day Pelican Island.

pilothouse: an enclosed place on the upper deck of a ship where the wheel is located.

powderhorn: a container used for carrying gunpowder and made by hollowing out the horn of a cow.

powder magazine: a place where gunpowder and explosives are stored.

powder monkey: the member of a ship's crew who was responsible for carrying powder charges from the magazine to the guns.

privateer: a privately owned warship, hired to attack enemy ships during time of war; also anyone who served on such ship.

ramrod: a rod used for ramming down the charge in a muzzle-loading gun.

recoil: the backward movement, or "kick," of a gun or cannon when it is fired.

rigging: the ropes, chains, etc. used in working the masts and sails on a ship.

saloon: the main cabin or dining area aboard a ship.

ship oars: to remove oars from water, or to place inside the boat.

sidewheel steamer: a steamboat propelled by large paddlewheels, located along each side.

71

skiff: a low, narrow rowboat.

skipper: slang term for the captain of a boat or ship.

speaking trumpet: a megaphone or funnel-shaped device for increasing the volume of a voice and directing it in a certain direction.

sternwheel: a steamboat propelled by a single, large paddle-wheel located at the stern.

Swift: (ship) One of two Baltimore-built privateers which sailed for the Republic of Texas. The other was the *Tom Toby.*

tarpaulin: a piece of canvas coated with a waterproofing compound.

thirty-two-pounder field gun: a cannon designed to be towed by horses and capable of firing a thirty-two-pound cannon-ball.

twenty-four-pounder: any cannon capable of firing a twenty-four-pound cannonball.

upperclassman: a student in his senior year at a military academy.

U.S. Revenue Service: original name for U.S. Coast Guard, the branch of service to which the *Harriet Lane* originally belonged.

vittles: slang for victual, an old term meaning food or provisions.

www.ingramcontent.com/pod-product-compliance
Lightning Source LLC
Chambersburg PA
CBHW061155040426
42445CB00013B/1691